SOCIAL WORKERS' EXPERIENCES OF

PARENTAL SUBSTANCE MISUSE

Julie Wilson

Social Work Monographs, Norwich
First Published 2007

Monograph No. 225

ISBN 978-1-85784-124-4

CONTENTS

LIST OF TABLES

I

INTRODUCTION

It is acknowledged that there has been very little research conducted in relation to professionals and more specifically, social workers' perceptions of working with children and families who are experiencing parental substance misuse. This is particularly evident within a Scottish context despite various studies highlighting the poor developmental and emotional effects of parental substance misuse on children and the Government's expectation that social workers will play a key role in responding to the needs of such families. As such this research sets out to explore children and families' Social Workers experiences of working with such families within a Scottish Local Authority and aims to give these workers a voice in this area of research.

Data were collected from Likert-style questionnaires and semi-structured interviews of 10 respondents and showed that social workers experienced difficulties in engaging and intervening in such families; lacked confidence in their knowledge of substance misuse, particularly in relation to drug use; felt that training provided was insufficient to carry out their role with such families and at times held derogatory attitudes towards such parents. Although we must be mindful of the small numbers used in this study the research concludes by attempting to identify how such findings may implicate current and future practice, particularly if such results are found to be commonplace amongst professionals and therefore recommends areas of future research to improve the situation.

Since the election of New Labour in 1997, dealing with substance misuse has been high on the political agenda (Adams et al 2002). This has also been reflected in the Scottish context with the devolution of the Scottish parliament (www.unison-scotland.org.uk) and the subsequent Scottish Executives' criminal justice plan *'Supporting Safer, Stronger Communities'* who reports that tackling drug misuse is a priority for *'ensuring public safety and reducing reoffending'* (www.scotland.gov.uk). It is well documented that people take substances for a variety of reasons, including the need to fit in with peers, escape social deprivation or to experience feelings of pleasure and release (May et al 2001). However it is also known that public opinion may not be sympathetic towards substance misuse with a recent Scottish Opinion Survey of 1001 adults, claiming that 76% of respondents strongly felt that those taking drugs were wasting their lives (Scottish Executive 2005). As such Gossop (2000:4) argues that those experiencing problem drug

use in society are often viewed as the stereotypical *'junkie'* who can be deemed as less deserving of help and resources than other citizens.

Once regarded as predominantly a health matter (www.hebs.scot.nhs.uk) which required treatment for a disease (Gossop 2000; Barber 2002), the agenda for tackling substance misuse has changed somewhat over recent years. It is now widely accepted that substance misuse should be addressed by not only treating the medical aspects of addiction but also by acknowledgement of how the social aspects of an individuals life may impact on and be impacted by an addiction problem (Kroll and Taylor 2003). As such professionals' roles have changed in the substance misuse arena, with other professions, including social work, having an equal responsibility in addressing the needs of substance misusing individuals and working in a multi-agency manner, at a co-ordinated, local level to effect change. Indeed social work are viewed as key stakeholders in *'safeguard(ing) the welfare of children who...live in families in which adults misuse drugs'* (Tackling Drugs in Scotland 1999) and have a responsibility to view such children as being *'in need'* according to s22 of the Children (Scotland) Act 1995 (Norrie 1998:59).

Current political debates surrounding substance misuse include the 2004 reclassification of cannabis from a class B drug to a class C under the Misuse of Drugs Act 1971 and the recent pilot of drug courts in Glasgow and Fife to utilise specific disposals such as Drug Testing and Treatment Orders (www.drugscope.org.uk). In terms of alcohol the Department of Health (DOH) in 1995 revised previous drinking limits from weekly limits to daily benchmarks of 3-4 units for men and 2-3 units for women with a few alcohol free days in between (cited in www.scotland.gov.uk). However a study by Lader et al (2000) into the impact of this found that only 2/3's of those surveyed had heard of daily benchmarks (cited in www.scotland.gov.uk). Among the recent trends in drinking in Scotland are the facts that women and young people are drinking more and that binge drinking, that is drinking more than twice the daily benchmarks, was on the increase (www.alcohol-focus-scotland.org.uk; www.news.bbc.co.uk). The Scottish Health Survey 1998 found that drinking had increased by 2% for women in the 16-24 age group between 1995-1998 and speculates that this is set to continue (www.show.scot.nhs.uk). In response the Scottish Executive launched their *'Plan for Action on Alcohol Problems'* with the primary aim of reducing drinking over the recommended limits by 2005 (www.isdscotland.org).

However the Government appear to be concentrating resources into dealing with drug taking and with the set up of the Scottish Drug Enforcement Agency (SDEA) in 2001 and the Antisocial Behaviour etc (Scotland) Act 2004 enabling police to shut down premises where drugs are believed to be in circulation, the pattern looks set to continue for some time (www.scotland.gov.uk). It is therefore notable that many Government publications have focused on drug misuse as opposed to alcohol misuse (ACMD 2000; Scottish Executive 2001; Scottish Executive 2002) despite the fact that Turnnard (2002a:7) asserts that *'(alcohol's) use affects more families than substance misuse'* with an estimated 1 million children affected by parental alcohol misuse. However in terms of drug misuse it is estimated that there are approximately 51456 individuals in Scotland who are misusing opiates or benzodiazepines (Hay et al 2004:15) and from this between 40800 and 58000 children are affected by parental drug misuse (ACMD 2000). Additionally recent figures show a dramatic rise in the number of drug related deaths, with the highest ever annual number of drug related deaths being reported in 2002 of 382 deaths (Scottish Executive 2003) and the number of clients seeking treatment has more than doubled from 2207 to 4689 in 2000 (DrugScope 2002) which has created further cause for concern. As such the Government have launched a national strategy *'Tackling Drugs in Scotland: Action in Partnership'* to address the four key aims of helping young people resist drug use; protecting communities from drug related crime; ensuring people receive treatment to overcome their drug problems and to intercept the availability of drugs on our streets (www.scotland.gov.uk/library/documents-w7/tdis-01.htm).

It appears clear then from the above that substance misuse is not only causing a great deal of concern to both the public and the Government but is also on the increase in Scotland and the UK as a whole. In this respect a great deal of focus has been on parents who misuse substances and agencies, including social work, have been charged with responding to parental substance misuse in a way that encompasses a multidisciplinary approach and early intervention (Protecting Children 1998; Scottish Executive 2001).

II

LITERATURE REVIEW

This literature review will focus on critically analysing literature relating to substance misuse within Scotland and the UK since 1990 in order to give a concise snapshot of the situation to date, proposing that focusing on an earlier period may be less relevant to the current misuse of alcohol and drugs. The initial intention was to focus on a Scottish perspective, appreciating how substance misuse may vary considerably from area to area, culture to culture, however English and USA research has been included to reflect the fact that a vast amount of research on the subject has been conducted in England as opposed to Scotland and to add depth to the study when certain topics were scarce in the UK. Literature was selected through searching Journal articles and the internet and through reviewing the bibliographies of other pieces of research. Issues relating to anti-discriminatory and anti-racist practice in relation to studies are interwoven throughout and major themes are highlighted. In order for clarity substance misuse will be defined as the use of alcohol or drugs which professionals, family members and the person feel is having a harmful affect on a person's life and those around them (Scottish Executive 2001:3).

Substance Misuse and Parenting

Klee (1998) in her review of past research, commented that being a parent and someone who misused substances is attributed with being *'selfish'* and *'irresponsible'* and discovered that public views of drug-using parents and judgemental attitudes of professionals, often acted as a deterrent for parents who misused substances to seek treatment. Kroll & Taylor (2003:246) warn that such *'...stereotypes often get in the way of being able to see what is happening and why...'* asserting that this will negatively impact on intervention.

Being a parent is a role that is associated with providing *'good enough'* parenting and providing a safe, secure environment for children is the expected standard (Every Child Matters 2003). Government publications and guidance for practitioners in dealing with substance misuse and families have argued that *'parents with drug problems need professionals to take responsibility for their children's welfare...'* detailing that *'parental use may have significant and damaging consequences for children'* (Scottish Executive 2001:1). It is therefore noted that much research appears to equate substance misuse with

drug misuse, with concern predominately focusing on the impact of parental substance misuse on children (McKeganey et al 2002; Barnard & McKeganey 2003; Meier et al 2004) and as such a plethora of research has been conducted in this area (Murray & Hogarth 2003; Hayden 2004; McInness & Newman 2005).

Research conducted by McKeganey et al (2002) and Barnard & McKeganey (2003) found similar themes relating to the negative impact of parental substance misuse on children. McKeganey et al's (2002) semi-structured interviews of 70 *'recovering heroin addicts'* (30 of whom were parents), in response to claims that substance misusing parents provide inconsistent, lukewarm care for children (Kandel 1990), found that in most of the interviews, drug use had a negative impact on parenting by suggesting *'maternal deprivation and neglect'* as parents spoke about monies being used to sustain drug use as opposed to caring for children. Similarly Barnard & McKeganey (2003) literature review on the subject identified that parents' *'preoccupation'* with drugs can often override the needs of their child, often resulting in the development of poor attachments and less parental supervision. Both studies commented on how parental drug use can lead to unstable family environments and disrupted household routines, with children sometimes taking on quasi-adult roles in caring for parents and siblings. McKeganey et al (2002) also voiced how children were often exposed to risks when accompanying parents to buy drugs, by being exposed to criminal behaviour when parents shoplifted or burgled to fund drug use or by people who frequented the home.

However we must view such results tentatively by considering the methodological weaknesses apparent. McKeganey et al (2002) study does not mention what steps were taken during the interview to minimise the possible affects the interviewers' presence may have had on the results, that is the *'Hawthorne Effect'* whereby people are aware of being interviewed and may not give a true account (Denscombe 2003:190) and thus it is important to appreciate how this may interplay with the results (Raymond 1996:62). It is also worth noting that McKeganey has been involved in other studies which perhaps do not show individuals who misuse substances in a positive light and has been fairly negative regarding social work involvement and therefore we must consider how bias may be evident in such studies (www.adoptionuk.com).

A similar study was that of McKeller & Coggans (1997) who explored the links between parental substance misuse and child behaviour. They showed how the development of problem behaviours such as drug misuse in young people, bad behaviour and poor school

outcomes was influenced by early socialisation and childhood experiences of living with parental substance misuse. However as both researchers come from medical background this may explain why they chose such a quantitative method for such an emotive subject as D'Cruz & Jones (2004:45) reminds us *'we understand our practice partly from our own assumptions...'* and their low response rate from their self-completion questionnaires (100 were sent to 38 agencies and only 40 were returned) is a good example of the disadvantage of such a method, sufficing caution is needed in terms of generalising from these results and how such methods may exclude those with literacy problems or other ethnicities from participation due to respondents having to read the questions.

Substance Misuse and Mothers/Fathers

In terms of differences in substance misuse between women and men, Neale's (2004) study of the relevance of gender in substance misuse discovered that there were not significant differences between men and women in terms of patterns of use but that there were stark differences between the sexes in various areas of their lives; for example it was noted that women were more likely to be dependent on state benefits and have more child care responsibilities than men. Similarly Greenfield et al (2003) revealed that previous research had shown that women also have shorter progressions from drug use to dependency than men and therefore may have more cause to hide their misuse due to childcare responsibilities, which perhaps reflects the ratio of women to men in treatment only being 1:3 (DOH 2000).

Thompson (2001) argues that parenting is often seen as mothering and as such a disproportionate number of studies have focused on mothers and the effects of substances on the unborn child. Women who misuse substances in society come under closer scrutiny and accountability, particularly when pregnant due to the risk of babies being born with either foetal alcohol syndrome (Turnnard 2002a) or neo-natal abstinence syndrome (www.edinburgh.gov.uk) all of which can make caring for such babies more difficult. Jones (2001) (cited in May et al 2001:155) states that this problem is exacerbated when women come from ethnic minority groups or lone parents, highlighting that they are doubly disadvantaged.

Nair et al (1997) claims that *'infants of substance abusing women are at an increased risk of receiving substitute care due to neglect/abuse or their mother's inability to care for them.'* Thus Barnard (2003) advocates that informal support offered by extended family

members can be crucial in keeping children *'safe and well in difficult times'* and other studies have commented on the supportive role grandparents play in providing stability to such families and avoiding the need for alternative care (Marcenko et al 2000; Barnard 2005).

Very few studies in the UK have researched fathering and substance misuse despite a literature review by the NHS arguing that men are more likely to drink above the recommended alcohol levels or have used illicit drugs in the last year, than women (Thom 2003) and are often named as the perpetrators of substance induced violence in children's accounts (Barnard & Barlow 2003).

Frank et al (2002) American study noted that fathers who misused substances were less likely to participate in their children's care-giving and remarked on how there is an increased risk of children being separated from their fathers through imprisonment. However vigilance must be applied with such findings due to the fact as interviewers read *'forced-choice'* questionnaires to women, they were relying on the accounts of these women as to the behaviour of men (Denscombe 2003:156). In contrast McMahon & Rounsville's (1997) literature review highlighted that we should avoid the negative stereotypes of such fathers being socially irresponsible and reports that various studies have found that fathers want to be involved as much as women, often feel the same guilt and shame in relation to their drug use and have been a source of support for pregnant mothers. The study also adds that although substance misusing fathers can have a negative impact on children, their total absence can be more detrimental.

Parental Substance Misuse and Child Protection

Various research has commented on the links between parental substance misuse and child protection (Scottish Executive 2001; Hayden 2004; Street et al 2004). Indeed Forrester's (2000) evaluation of social workers' case conference reports of 50 families with 95 children on the Child Protection Register in an inner London Social Services Department in 1994, found that there was a strong correlation between emotional abuse, heroin misuse and registration for neglect and that such children were also more likely to be involved in care proceedings. Forrester (2000) also commented that social workers involved in the study appeared to have a familiarity with alcohol and viewed it as a contributory factor to other social problems, whereas their lack of knowledge of heroin lead them to see heroin *as the problem* rather than a mitigating factor.

Forrester (2000) findings should be viewed with prudence as *'secondary analysis'* was used to analyse case records after they had been recorded by someone else, which not only opens the potential for issues to be taken out of context or findings misinterpreted (Alston & Bowles 2003:188) but is also arguably an oppressive research method as it fails to give the subjects of the research a voice (Thompson 2000a:60). Nevertheless such findings are consistent with Neale (2004) who found that information from Glasgow City Council demonstrated that problem drug or alcohol use was the underlying reasons for inclusion on the Child Protection Register for 52% of cases.

However Sloan (1998) argues that *'child maltreatment'* and child protection procedures are not always associated with parental substance misuse and a study by Hill et al (1996) (cited in Sloan 1998) found that children's reactions to parental drinking sometimes had positive reactions with children reporting increased generosity and humour from parents. Therefore Garbarino (1995) stresses that an accumulation of risk factors, including less income, poor housing and poor supports, gives rise to child care concerns as opposed to substance misuse alone.

Parental Substance Misuse and Resilience

Despite the fact that Kearney et al (2000) highlight that most studies focus on risk and the negative effects of substance misuse, many publications have commented on how children of substance misusing parents can overcome adversity (Hogan 1998; ACMD 2000; Murray & Hogarth 2003).

It is said that the presence of sufficient income, a consistent caring adult, regular attendance at school and intelligence are all factors that can protect children against negative outcomes (Howe 1995; Scottish Executive 2001). A number of studies have mentioned the strategies parents (mainly mothers) have taken in order to minimise any negative effects their substance misuse has on their children (Nair et al 1997; Klee 1998; Barnard 2003). Barker & Carson (1999) who used participant observation and semi-structured interviews of 17 substance misusing women to explore their experiences of mothering, found that the women viewed themselves as good mothers when they protected their children from harm and fulfilled their child's physical needs and felt guilty when they failed to protect their children, recognising the risks their children could be exposed to. Most women attempted to achieve this as often as possible and such findings were also

echoed by Street et al (2004) who found that such parents wanted the best for their children. However, it is important to acknowledge that as Barker & Carson (1999) study is American, there is a danger that it may reflect differing social structures appreciating that the American drug of choice appears to be crack/cocaine as opposed to heroin in the UK.

Although such findings may contradict previous aforementioned studies that link parental substance misuse and poor outcomes for children, there is still concern about the links between parental substance misuse and child welfare as evidenced by the Caleb Ness Inquiry (www.edinburgh.gov.uk) and government guidelines which remind us that *'children...being born into drug misusing families...their protection must be a priority'* (Tackling Drugs in Scotland 1999).

The Voices of Children

A growing number of studies are beginning to highlight the detrimental affects of parental substance misuse from a child's perspective. Kroll's (2004) content analysis of seven published studies which featured accounts from children and young adults about growing up with either drug or alcohol problems and Barnard & Barlow (2003) 2 year qualitative study of 36 children and young people found similar emerging themes from the children's accounts. Both studies discovered that secrecy was commonplace with children often employing strategies such as avoiding taking friends home to conceal their parents' substance misuse and that they often knew from an early age not to 'tell' anyone about their family situation for fear of what might happen. Furthermore both showed accounts of children trying to mediate between family members when violence occurred and not attending school for worrying about parents. Loss of childhood was a theme in many of the studies Kroll (2004) reviewed, whilst Barnard & Barlow revealed that children felt torn between loyalties to their parents, feeling *'different from other people',* which then led children to develop problems with their sense of self and socialising with peers (Barnard & Barlow 2003).

As the respondents are not interviewed directly in Kroll's (2004) research we have to acknowledge the possibility of bias due to the researchers choosing the topics to search in content analysis (Silverman 2000) and thus consider the possibility that such research may be imbued with the researchers' values (D'Cruz & Jones 2004:45). Similarly in Barnard & Barlow (2003) study because they are sometimes relying on accounts from young adults

(up to 22 years old) who are talking about childhood, there may be hazed accounts or discrepancies which should be considered.

The Role of Social Work

In relation to parental substance misuse and its impact on children, the Government have published a number of key policy/guidance documents placing responsibility on the role of social workers and other key professionals to jointly assess risk/need with the introduction of the new Framework for the Assessment of Children in Need and their Families (www.basw.co.uk) and emphasise the need for early intervention in families where substance misuse is problematic (Protecting Children 1998; Scottish Executive 2001). Similarly high profile public inquiries such as the Caleb Ness Inquiry, where 11 week old Caleb died from shaking injuries after being allowed to go home unsupervised with his mother who had substance misuse problems and had previous children removed from her care due to this and a father who had an acquired brain injury and previous convictions for drugs and assault, demonstrated again the dangers of how parental substance misuse can act as a cumulative factor to a child's *'avoidable death'*. Caleb was placed on the Child Protection Register but no other formal review of risk took place when the baby went home. Such cases has fuelled the need for social workers and other professionals to respond to parental substance misuse effectively (www.edinburgh.gov.uk/socialwork/calebness/calebness.html).

Although the overall feel of the guidance appears derogatory towards substance misusing parents by focusing on risk, the Government publication *'Getting Our Priorities Right'* (Scottish Executive 2001:29) advocates that although professionals should bear in mind how hard parents may try to conceal substance use, that they should also endeavour to work in partnership with parents by adopting an open and honest approach, stressing that *'parents with problem drug use should be assessed like other parents'*. Indeed the Scottish Social Services Council (SSSC 2003:Code 5.5) Codes of Practice supports this by emphasising that social workers should not *'discriminate unlawfully...against service users...'* and should display core social work values of respecting individuals (Banks 2001).

Kroll and Taylor (2003:255) advocate that assessment must take a holistic approach, promoting the use of Prochaska and DiClemente's Transtheoretical Model of Addiction (Barber 2002) and Motivational Interviewing (Miller & Rollnick 2002) by social workers

to help people move through the process of change. Similarly Barnard (2005) believes that taking a family perspective is paramount, with Turnnard (2002b) stressing that practitioners must remember that most parents want what's best for their children and that building on strengths is as important as focusing on problems. However Corby (1996) (cited in Kemshall & Pritchard 1996:16) reminds us that assessing such risk/need, especially agreeing upon acceptable standards, is very difficult to do. Perhaps surprisingly then, there is very little research exploring the views of professionals in this area despite the fact that McInnes & Newman (2005) in their interviews with practitioners, including social work, found that a high proportion of their caseloads (50%+) had children who were deemed to be *'at risk'* from their parents substance misuse problems.

Substance misuse is described as a *'complex and growing problem'* (Tackling Drugs in Scotland 1999), those studies which have focused on social workers' experiences of working with such families reveal that professionals have dilemmas in engaging with families because of their fear of what intervention would bring if children were involved; difficulties establishing trust due to the secrecy and denial that substance misuse often created; worrying about assessing risk for fear of either over or under reacting to the problem (Taylor & Kroll 2004) and of not knowing what *'good enough'* parenting was (Kroll and Taylor 2003:243). Indeed research carried out by Hayden (2004) into concerns amongst social workers about parental substance misuse, confirmed that a high proportion of the 47 social workers participating reported finding it hard to support families when they refused help for fear of their children being removed and felt out of their depth in understanding the substance misuse needs of parents, with a minority admitting that they did not have faith in such parents changing.

Such feelings were echoed in research by Watson et al (2004) who found that confidence and knowledge levels amongst health and social care staff with regards to substance misuse varied, with most feeling more confident in dealing with alcohol issues as opposed to drug issues, which perhaps reflects the social acceptability of alcohol in our culture. This equally may have implications for intervention and would agree with the recent *'21st Century Social Work Review'* which acknowledged that social work is a profession under pressure, *'lacking in confidence and not delivering their full potential'* (Scottish Executive 2006). Similarly research carried out by Duffy et al (1995) into whether social workers who had been trained along with their line managers, felt more supported in the work place, discovered that whilst training did increase social workers' knowledge and confidence in their roles (Role Adequacy) and did increase their feelings of adequacy in

their role and right to intervene (Role Legitimacy), that this diminished after a period of time particularly if they did not receive support from their seniors (Role Support) (Watson et al 2003).

Substance Misuse, Structural Causes and Disadvantaged Groups

Hogan (1998) research reminds us that it is not drug use *per se* that impacts on children but rather the presence of other social stressors such as lone parent-hood, mental health problems, debt etc. Studies have discovered that many parents who misused substances have histories of sexual abuse and poor educational attainment (Nair 1997; Turnnard 2002b; Neale 2004) and suggest that such individuals take substances to escape emotional pain (Sloan 1998). Street et al's (2004) research of 68 drug using women and a control group of 127 non-drug using women, found that those women who misused substances and had low social economic backgrounds were more likely to have children who entered the child protection system than those who were misusing substances but had more stable backgrounds, suggesting that drug use alone is not always responsible for poor outcomes.

Therefore a number of studies have reported how themes such as poverty, deprivation and disadvantage feature in the lives of people who misuse substances (Plant et al 2005, Meier et al 1999). Alcock (1997) reminds us that certain groups in society, such as ethnic minorities and disabled people, are more susceptible to poverty than others and it is thus argued that such people may be more vulnerable to substance misuse due to their social positioning and the discrimination they face (www.drugscope.org.uk; www.drugs.gov.uk). However despite the Race Relations (Amendment) Act 2000 stating that services have a duty to provide for the needs of ethnic minority groups, most research in this area has tended to come from England and the US with some suggesting that gaps in the research are due to such groups remaining hidden due to stigma of substance misuse (www.scotland.gov.uk).

However research conducted in the UK by Bakshi et al (2004) into substance misuse amongst 16-24 year old Chinese, Indian and Pakistani young people and their parents in Glasgow and a literature review by Fountain et al's (2003) on ethnic minorities and substance misuse in England, found that substance misuse, in particular drug use, was not just a white problem but also existed in such communities. Around 1/5 of the communities in Bakshi et al (2004) study admitted to having used cannabis in the past and Fountain et al (2003) literature review found that ethnic minority communities reasons behind taking

substances was similar to the white population, that is; peer influence and to fit in. Both studies commented on how culture played a part in sustaining or condoning drug use, with parents and older generations stressing that they would view their child's drug use as bringing shame on the family and therefore overwhelmingly reported that young people often concealed their drug use. The studies therefore highlighted that services needed to be sensitive to the culture and language needs of such communities and agreed that the belief that such families often liked to deal with problems themselves was a misconception.

With regards to disability, Li & Ford (1998), in their American study, found during their random sample of 900 women with disabilities, that such women used drugs for the same reason as other non-disabled women, that is, social isolation, peer influence and mental health issues. Similarly Dyter & Mitchell (2003) literature review revealed that people with disabilities are more likely to encounter problems with personal adjustment, normalisation, socialisation and discrimination because of their disability which may place them more at risk of misusing substances. There appears however to be no studies in the UK on substance misuse and disability, despite it being acknowledged that disabled individuals often have easier access to prescription drugs than the general population and current debates about legalising cannabis for MS sufferers shows that drug use within this community is happening (www.drugs.gov.uk). The US studies that have been conducted often use quantitative methods, such as questionnaires to conduct the studies, meaning that we are lacking the voices of these individuals, which may be more evident in the case of disabled-ethnic minority people who may be doubly disadvantaged by this (Payne 1997:7).

Summary

In conclusion the themes emerging from the literature overwhelmingly report on the poor developmental and emotional effects of parental substance misuse on children and the role professionals should have in early intervention and assessing the harm children may face. Furthermore much of the government literature appears to advocate for a surveillance approach from professionals with the need for continuous assessment and monitoring of the situation and for parents to be challenged about their drug use. This may at times cause conflict between professionals duty to work in partnership with parents where possible, and contradicts the pieces of research which has shown that parents try to protect their children from their drug use. There is an obvious lack of research on ethnic minority or other disadvantaged groups and it is also apparent that much of the research took a gendered perspective, particularly in the case of children whereby mothers were often the

focus of the study. Very few studies focused on professional, or indeed social workers' perceptions of such families and as such their voices are missing in the research despite them being a central player in responding to the needs of such families.

III

RESEARCH DESIGN AND METHODOLOGY

Focus of the study/rationale

The focus of the study will concentrate on Social Workers' experience of parental substance misuse in a Children and Families setting. The rationale for targeting substance misuse, which includes alcohol as well as drugs, was due to an interest I developed on the subject area whilst on placement in an addiction service. Denscombe (2003) asserts that choosing a subject area which is interesting to the researcher is an important component of conducting research. The specific focus on parental substance misuse derived from the fact that whilst out on placement in a Children and Families area team it became apparent that social workers often appeared frustrated at the apparent 'chaotic' nature of such families and therefore made the occasional discriminatory comment towards such parents. Similarly as we have seen from the literature review, tackling parental substance misuse is high on the political agenda with practice becoming entrenched with minimising the detrimental effects of parental misuse on children and as such there is a clear expectation on professionals working with parental substance misuse to intervene and protect children's welfare (Scottish Executive 2001; ACMD 2000). Therefore as social workers have been identified as having a central role in assessing and responding to the needs of families who misuse substances (Norrie 1998:200), it was felt that an exploration of their experiences would *facilitate the voices'* of such workers (D'Cruz & Jones 2004:128) and open up an area of research that is currently under-researched. Witkin (1995:427) highlights *'the social work profession...ha(s) a unique commitment to a contextual understanding of people...'* and it is felt that an understanding of social workers' experiences, is equally important (cited in D'Cruz & Jones 2004:17).

Objectives of the study

The main focus of the study was therefore to:

Explore Social Workers' experiences of working with parents who misuse substances and their children, in a Children and Families Setting.

Within the main aim of the study the following sub-objectives were addressed:

- To discover the experiences of social workers towards the subject area.
- From this to determine as far as possible social workers' attitudes surrounding parental substance misuse.
- To ascertain whether such experiences and attitudes on the whole are positive or negative and suggest how this may impact on practice.

Such objectives and sub-objectives were expected to reflect the findings of the literature review which suggests that social workers may experience difficulties in practising with parents who misuse substances (Taylor & Kroll 2004) and may in turn have the potential to develop derogatory attitudes to such families (Hayden 2004).

Research Design

Case Study

D'Cruz & Jones (2004:83) assert *'the choice of design is driven by the research question'*, therefore as the purpose of the research question is to explore the under-researched experiences of social workers, a case study design was considered appropriate (Denscombe 2003:32). The advantage of using this was that it would allow an in depth, retrospective study to be conducted in the natural setting of the office environment, which would hopefully enable participants to feel more at ease with the process and facilitate further involvement. Furthermore as the research was small-scale with the aim of *'illuminat(ing) the general by looking at the particular'* a case study was felt appropriate especially as it enabled multiple methods to be used to answer the research question (Denscombe 2003:30). A 'case' in this study will be defined as a Children and Families Area Team in a Scottish Local Authority and the unit of analysis will compromise of the Senior Social Workers and Social Workers who work within the 'case'.

It is acknowledged that a disadvantage of the case study design may be the question of how representative the study can be. However there will be no claim of generalisation from the study and although each case is unique, it is also a single example of a broader class of things (Yin 1994) and thus the findings can be viewed in respect of other areas but will have to be treated with caution appreciating that different areas have differing cultures, geography and practices (Hay et al 2004).

Methods

It was initially thought that a purely qualitative approach, using the interview method to illicit information from interviewees, in order to *'yield rich insights into people's...experiences...attitudes and feelings'* (May 2001:120) would best suit the research question. Indeed Feminist researchers have stated that women respond better when there is personal connection between themselves and the researcher (Raymond 1996).

However realising how difficult it may be to ascertain attitudes from respondents using only interviews due to the sensitive subject of parental substance misuse and also the possible ways the presence of the interviewer may interrupt the process (*'Halo Effect/Hawthorne Effect'*) (Denscombe 2003:190), it was decided that a mixed-method approach, using both quantitative and qualitative methods, would enable the question to be answered more effectively as methods could complement each other and cancel out each other's negative effects (D'Cruz & Jones 2004:122).

A questionnaire was used to collect information for analysis in order to discover general knowledge and attitudes of social workers in relation to substance misuse (May 1993). This was a self-completion questionnaire encompassing a five-point, Likert Scale meaning that respondents had to choose between the categories on the scale, ranging from strongly agree through to strongly disagree, for each statement to decide which answer best applied to them. A Likert Scale was decided as the best method to answer this part of the research question due to the recognition of its suitability for gauging attitudes (Kumar 1996) and was adapted from the Drug and Drug Problems Perceptions Questionnaire (DDPPQ) which was originally designed to measure mental health professionals' attitudes to working with drug users (Watson et al 2003). However it is noted how this method may oppress groups such as women or ethnic minority individuals who are denied a voice by being forced to choose between answers which may not reflect their opinion; and Feyerbend (1975) (cited in Thompson 2000a:48) reminds us that such a purely positive approach is not only incorrectly characterised as value-free but also ignores issues such as race, poverty and gender.

Therefore semi-structured interviews were used to gather information about experiences and empower voices to be heard. The interview schedule was drafted using the themes from the literature and although appreciating how this could direct the interview, they were

only used as a guide, with emphasis being placed on flexibility as interviewees decided on the order of topics discussed and had the opportunity to develop ideas. Although unstructured interviews may be seen as more empowering it was decided not to use this method due to the importance of keeping the research focused because of the obvious taxes on the social workers' time and the researcher's inexperience of conducting research.

As the methods were used to collect differing perspectives of the research question, the process of *'triangulation'* was used in order to corroborate the findings of both methods against previous literature, which can be found in the comment and critique of the research findings. It is hoped that the application of such a process would not only add to the amount of knowledge about the subject area but also aid in the research being treated with greater validity and objectivity (Denscombe 2003:133).

Ethics

Ethical approval was sought from Glasgow Caledonian University before conducting the research and three principles were taken into account in order to ensure ethical practice and meet with the BASW Code of Ethics for Social Work (Denscombe 2003:136):

Principle 1 – The interests of participants should be protected

In order to gain access to the organisation and discuss issues of confidentiality, meetings were held with the Acting Director of Social Work for the Scottish Local Authority and the Children and Families Head of Department appreciating that such people would be the main gatekeepers to the organisation and had the power to permit the research going ahead (Handy 1993). Such meetings enabled access to the organisation, approval of the topic of research and ways the research should be progressed to be agreed and granted. Permission was given to contact senior social workers in the first instance to discuss how they would like the research to progress and issues of confidentiality were agreed in conjunction with the Data Protection Act 1998 (Baillie et al 2003) that is, that the information collected from participants would only be used for the purpose of the research, would be stored safely and destroyed after it was no longer needed for the research process. Similarly it was agreed that all information received from respondents would be confidential with no-one being identified.

Principle 2 – Research should avoid deception or misrepresentation

All those who took part in the process were treated with an open and honest approach, were fully informed with an information sheet about the aims of the research, that is, to gather experiences of the participants as well as their attitudes and given the choice about whether to continue.

Principle 3 – Participants should give informed consent

In the information sheet participants were also advised that their information would be kept confidential, being destroyed after use and were asked to sign the form giving their informed consent to participating in the research with the understanding that their participation was voluntary and could be withdrawn at any point.

As *'the researcher's identity, values and beliefs cannot be entirely eliminated from the process...'* (Denscombe 2003:268), it was acknowledged that attention would have to be paid to the researcher's positioning in relation to the research. As a 27 year old white, female who currently works in the Children and Families Area Team of the Local Authority where the research was conducted, it was important to exercise sufficient control over the research process by 1) piloting questionnaires and interviews for any inherent biases to revealed prior to the research; 2) consulting with participants about the research process and discussions of findings; 3) using mixed-methods to counteract the possible bias inherent in each method. Care was also taken with regards to how the researcher's age, sex, race, gender and ethnicity impacted on the research process, although it was also felt that the use of self was also positive as this enabled engaging with respondents and facilitating the voices of those usually marginalised in research, for example women to be possible.

Sample

In fitting with the case study design of the research, respondents were selected for the study using non-probability, purposive sampling. This decision was taken because such sampling is deemed appropriate when there is no need to include large numbers in the research and when the researcher knows something about the people to be included in the study and thus deliberately selects them in order to provide the most valuable data (Denscombe 2003:15). It is appreciated that purposive sampling has the potential for bias

and does not have the benefit of being generalised like random sampling, however measures were taken as mentioned in the ethical section to counteract such bias.

The population was the Local Authority's Children and Families' Area Teams which the sample was drawn from and one team was used as the sample as it was identified by management as the most likely to have more instances of social workers working with parental substance misuse due to being situated in a more densely populated town area. The sample consisted of approximately 4 senior social workers and 18 social workers and it was decided to focus on such workers' experiences because of their statutory responsibility and accountability to such families. However this was not to deny the dedicated work of social work assistants or other elements of social work who also deal with such families but as Marlow (2001:132) highlights *'you cannot include everyone in the study.'*

Respondents were recruited by the researcher attending team meetings and asking individuals to volunteer for the process. However although a conscious effort was made to recruit male respondents in order to avoid the research becoming sexist, this became difficult due to their small numbers. As such snowball sampling was used to recruit 1 male social work assistant with considerable experience, which gave a more balanced perspective in terms of gender (Denscombe 2003).

In total, 10 participants took part in the research process which consisted of 7 social workers, 1 social work assistant and 2 senior social workers. The mix was 4 males to 6 females, which effectively is a ratio of 2:3 and provided a wealth of insight into the topic. However as no member of staff was of minority ethnic origin or disabled it was acknowledged that there is consequently a distinct lack of such perceptions in the research.

Implementation of the Research

Participatory Approach

Appreciating that *'people are and always will be expert on themselves'* (Smale et al 2000:137) and that research is *'embedded in power relationships between the researcher and the researched'* (D'Cruz & Jones 2004:131) it was felt important to approach the research from a stance that gave the respondents as much control as possible over the study. As such a participatory approach, which maximised the respondents' opportunity to

be included in the research process was adopted (Cornwell & Jewkes 1995). This was particularly important considering that the researcher also worked in the organisation, appreciating that it was paramount to consider ways in which her own self may influence the process and thus helped even out any power imbalances (Denscombe 2003:170).

In essence the participatory approach is underpinned by the ethos of *'respect for the person'* (Banks 2001:24) as participants are seen to be able to understand their own situation and develop and analyse solutions. Cornwall and Jewkes (1995) state that participation is normally partial and argue that participation should be seen as part of a continuum. They provide a 4-stage continuum which begins at *'contractual'* where respondents are co-opted into the research process, *'consultive'* where participants are asked for their opinions before intervention takes place, *'collaborative'* where the project respondents and the researcher work together on initiatives managed and designed by the researcher and *'collegiate'* (emancipatory) where the subjects of the research would work as partners being included in determining the area of research.

Whilst it would have been ideal to work from the emancipatory level, only the *'collaborative'* level was possible due to the research having to be negotiated with senior managers before it was allowed to go ahead. Thus participants were excluded from the initial stages of negotiating and agenda setting but were involved by:

- Being consulted on the topic of the research and of its particular interest to them.
- They were asked where and when they wanted the questionnaires/interviews to take place and how they would like the process to proceed.
- As such all respondents were given the questionnaires and interview schedules beforehand and were given the opportunity to comment on the contents, allowing them the opportunity to change certain questions which they were not happy with and decide on how they wanted the data to be collected.
- Once both methods had been analysed, respondents were each given a summary of their research findings and encouraged to comment on whether they thought this was a fair reflection of what they said.

The aim was to make the research process as transparent as possible and to work alongside the participants to enhance their empowerment, to gain their truth of the topic area and increase reliability of the research findings.

Data Collection Methods

Each of the 10 respondents was given a Likert-style questionnaire to complete and a one-to-one semi-structured interview with the researcher. As both methods were used to answer different aspects of the research question it was deemed appropriate for the questionnaire to be completed first, whilst the researcher was present which gave the added benefit of counteracting low response rates and enabling any confusions to be explained (May 2001), followed by the interview. This helped avoid the possibility of the interview influencing responses in the questionnaire.

The questionnaires and interviews took place in the social work department, in interview rooms, which the respondents decided on and the process lasted between 50 minutes to an hour and a half in each case. Both data collection methods were piloted beforehand with the aim of not only giving the research a higher degree of reliability (D'Cruz & Jones 2004) but also enabled the researcher to become aware of power imbalances present in the data collection process and thus tailor the approach. For example, piloting ensured that the researcher remembered to provide a coherent explanation of the research process and remind respondents of their right to leave the process at any time, making the research more empowering.

During interviews, open-questions were used where possible in order to allow participants to decide on the wording used, the length of their discussion and the subject matter which aided collection of the full richness and complexity of their views (Denscombe 2003). Respondents were given a clear definition of what substance misuse meant in the context of the research process and the researcher employed skills such as paraphrasing (Trevithick 2000:94) and adopting the SOLER approach to engaging, that is face the person Squarely; adopt an Open posture; Lean towards the person; maintain good Eye contact and be Relaxed, in order to set participants at ease (Egan 2002:88).

Interviews were audio-recorded, after asking permission from respondents, in order to provide a permanent record of the discussions and to avoid disrupting the flow of the interview by attempting to write what was said. However it was acknowledged that a particular disadvantage of such method was that non-verbal communication and contextual factors may be missed (Denscombe 2003:177) and as such field notes were also taken, where permitted, during the interviews. Respondents were also given the opportunity to decide whether they wanted to add anything at the end of each section of the interview.

Analytical Methods

Questionnaires were pre-coded before being given to respondents in two ways. Firstly questions were placed into categories which were predetermined by the DDPPQ under the headings of: Role Adequacy (referring to whether practitioners felt adequately prepared for their role in terms of knowledge and skills), Role Legitimacy (which refers to what practitioners feel is their responsibility in their role and right to interfere) and Role Support (relates to the support practitioners feel they receive from colleagues to help them perform their role). It is deemed that the presence of these factors will enhance worker's motivation, self-esteem and satisfaction in working with such groups (Watson et al 2003).

Secondly questionnaires were pre-coded on the basis that the lower the overall score of respondents the more positive their attitude to substance misuse was deemed. The questionnaire was split into two sections: one for alcohol and one for drugs with 18 questions in each and responses ranged from 1 – 5, that is from strongly agree through to strongly disagree. Certain questions were worded negatively or worded differently to avoid participants following a set pattern to filling in the questionnaire and to encourage them to think about their responses, thus giving a truer account of their feelings.

It was determined that a score of 108 or above was particularly negative due to the fact that if each respondent chose a neutral score (that is, a 3 showing that they did not agree nor disagree with the statement) all the way through the questionnaire then the lowest score they could get in each section without being either negative or positive would be 54 and 108 in total, therefore these scores were used as bench marks to analyse the questionnaires.

Analysis of the questionnaires used descriptive univariate statistics at a nominal and ordinal level due to the fact that a Likert scale was the type of questionnaire chosen. Analysis occurred in two phases, first questionnaires were analysed by each question in each of the DDPPQ sections to look for frequencies and patterns (Alston & Bowles 2003:223). Secondly in order to add depth to analysis, questionnaires were totalled for each respondent to give overall scores for each section and ultimately to ascertain whether they had a negative or positive attitude to drugs or alcohol and compared against nominal data such as age and length of training to ascertain whether there were any correlations between variables.

However it is recognised that using ordinal data cannot give us the *'cause'* of why people have chosen a certain category or by how much they differ in their responses (Denscombe 2003:241) and therefore this is where the importance of cross-referencing with qualitative data became apparent in the process.

Audio-recordings from the semi-structured interviews were transcribed by the researcher and combined with any field-notes to enable the researcher to *'get inside the data'* much more easily and to assist with the analysis process (Morse & Richards 2002). Recordings were transcribed as verbatim as possible; although this was extremely time-consuming, the realisation that people do not speak in succinct sentences and thus transcripts need to punctuated to be readable, reinforced the need to minimise the possibility of bias entering the process and enabled data to remain as 'raw' as possible (Denscombe 2003).

Once the interviews had been transcribed and field notes added to them, the process of data reduction (Kumar 1996:257) then began by looking for *'patterns and processes, commonalities and differences'* in the transcripts, which were then categorised in order to identify important themes (Denscombe 2003:272). Topics were then organised around themes which flowed through the participants' responses and listed within a separate document with accompanying pieces of text in order to illustrate the theme. This process continued until themes were *'saturated'* and no more could be identified (Kumar 1996:257). Once themes had been gathered each were analysed in order to ascertain their interconnections with other themes and provide possible explanations as to why they existed.

Only those themes which were important to the research process that is, those which answered the particular research question/objectives and which reflected the findings of the literature review, were included in the findings, appreciating that Morse & Richards (2002:136) argue that themes must be selected with a purpose and relevant to the project.

IV

THE RESEARCH FINDINGS

Findings should be viewed in light of the fact that the local authority was without an appropriate drug resource for a few months before the research took place, had not had a training manager for some time and that both the Getting Our Priorities Right protocols (Scottish Executive 2001) and Framework for the Assessment of Children in Need and their Families (www.basw.co.uk), were not fully rolled out when the research was conducted. Furthermore, the small scale nature of the research means that the following findings must be treated tentatively and are not necessarily indicative of all Children and Families' social work teams.

Findings of the questionnaires

Pre-coded Findings based on the DDPPQ Questionnaire

Role Adequacy

Refers to how equipped respondents feel in relation to their knowledge base in carrying out their role.

- In terms of having a working knowledge of substances, respondents appeared more confident with their knowledge of alcohol use compared to drug use. 6 out of 10 respondents agreed that they had enough knowledge of drugs (3 were unsure), compared to 1 out of the 10 respondents strongly agreeing and 6 agreeing (only 1 respondent was unsure) with alcohol.

- In terms of knowing enough about the risk of developing such problems there seemed to be a slightly higher number of respondents feeling more knowledgeable about this in relation to drugs with 6 out of 10 feeling they knew enough about the risks of drugs, compared to 4 out of 10 for risks in alcohol.

- It appeared that respondents felt more assured in advising service users about the effects of alcohol in their role, with 5 out of 10 respondents agreeing that they would feel able to appropriately advise service users about the effects of alcohol, compared to only 3 out of 10 in drugs. They were also more satisfied in working with alcohol misuse than drug misuse, as although 6 people felt unsure about being

satisfied with their work with alcohol misuse, only 2 people disagreed with the statement compared to 5 out of 10 being unsure with drugs and 4 disagreeing.

Role Legitimacy

Refers to how respondents feel they have the right to intervene or the extent to which they view certain aspects of their work as their responsibility.

- With regards to feeling comfortable about asking service users about their substance misuse it appeared that respondents felt more comfortable asking about drug problems as opposed to alcohol problems with 9 people out of 10 agreeing with this statement in terms of drug use, compared to 7 out of 10 with alcohol use. No-one disagreed in the drug section about having to do this, whereas 1 person did in the alcohol section.

- However in comparison, there was a slight suggestion that respondents felt they had more right to ask about any aspect of a service users' alcohol use opposed to their drug use with 2 out of 10 respondents either strongly agreeing/agreeing with this statement with regards to drugs and 4 out of the 10 disagreeing; however although 2 people out of 10 either strongly agreed/agreed with this statement in terms of alcohol, 3 out of the 10 disagreed.

Motivation

Refers to respondents' perceived willingness or motivation to work with those who misuse substances.

- In general respondents claimed to be more interested in the nature of drugs and the responses to it, with 7 out of 10 respondents either strongly agreeing/agreeing with this statement about drugs compared to 4 out of 10 with alcohol.

- However, in terms of whether they felt there was little they could do to help those with problem alcohol or drug use, although most respondents either strongly disagreed/disagreed with this statement in both accounts, a slight difference did show as 1 respondent agreed with this in relation to drugs as opposed to no-one doing so with alcohol.

- Respondents appeared ambivalent about intervention as when asked whether they felt that the best they could do with someone who had a drug or alcohol problem was to refer them onto someone else, although 5 out of the 10 either strongly

disagreed/disagreed with this statement, 5 out of the 10 being were also unsure in both alcohol and drugs sections.

Task-specific Self Esteem

Refers to how respondents feel with regards to their work with those who misuse substances.

- Overall most people disagreed with the statement of having less respect for those who misused drugs or alcohol. However of those who agreed it would appear that they had less respect for those who misused drugs with 2 out of 10 agreeing compared to 1 out of 10 agreeing for alcohol.

- Although in general respondents claimed to feel competent about the work they did with those who misused substances, there was evidence that they felt slightly more assured in their role with alcohol misuse than drugs. When asked whether they felt no good at times when working with such client groups, 6 out of 10 either strongly disagreed/disagreed with this statement and 3 were unsure in terms of alcohol, compared to 5 out of 10 and 4 being unsure with regards to drugs.

Work Satisfaction

Refers to how respondents enjoy working with those who misuse substances.

- When asked about whether they wanted to work with those who misused drugs or alcohol, most respondents failed to commit on this statement with the majority marking their answer as unsure in both cases. Only 3 out of 10 respondents agreed with this statement about drugs and 2 out of 10 in the alcohol section, perhaps suggesting that more wanted to work with drug misuse, however 2 respondents in both sections disagreed with the statement, suggesting that the preference not to work with such users, was the same for both drugs and alcohol.

- Respondents seemed to feel that it was more rewarding to work with problem alcohol use as only 1 out of the 10 respondents agreed that it was rewarding to work with drug users, compared to 2 out of 10 for alcohol use. Again most chose to mark unsure as their answer in both sections.

- In terms of feeling as if they understood problem drug and alcohol use the majority of respondents were unsure in both alcohol and drug use as 6 out of 10 marked unsure in both cases.

Summary

In terms of Role Adequacy and Role Legitimacy it could be argued that these elements were low amongst respondents, particularly in relation to drug use. This was evidenced by the fact that overall respondents appeared to feel they had poor knowledge and confidence in relation to substances, especially in relation to drug use and thus felt more satisfied in working with alcohol misuse. Although perhaps surprisingly, respondents were more confident with their knowledge of risks with drugs but showed that they felt they had more right and thus were more comfortable with asking about an individual's alcohol use.

Therefore the fact that Role Adequacy and Role Legitimacy were low, specifically in relation to drug misuse, appeared also to be reflected in respondents Motivation, Self-esteem and Work Satisfaction. Although respondents appeared to have a positive attitude and thus be motivated towards working with those who misused substances, it was clear that despite this, they also seemed to be less sure about helping those who had drug problems compared to those with alcohol problems and equally lacked confidence in intervening with both drug and alcohol problems. Similarly in terms of Self-esteem and Work Satisfaction, both appeared to be low in general but again more so in relation to drug misuse. Respondents appeared to display that they had respect for working with such service users but showed less respect for drug users, with a higher proportion being more assured to working with alcohol than drugs. Furthermore although respondents in Work Satisfaction seemed to be fairly non-committal, it would appear however that when respondents did answer, there was a slight preference for wanting to work and feeling it rewarding to work with those who misused alcohol rather than drugs.

Findings of Questionnaires – Compared to nominal data

As aforementioned, overall scores of respondents for the questionnaire for both the drugs and alcohol sections were deemed to be positive if they fell below 108, 54 in each section. Overall scores of respondents ranged from 76 (most positive) to 111 (least positive).

Table 1

Individual Scores for Alcohol and Drugs

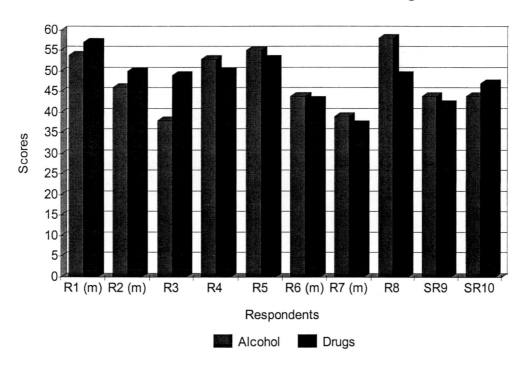

*Note – (m) stands for male respondents and SR stands for senior respondents

As can be seen from the above graph, respondents seemed to score pretty similar in both sections of the questionnaire, suggesting that if they had a positive attitude to drugs by having a low score, they would have a pretty similar score in the alcohol section.

Surprisingly in terms of overall scores there appeared to be slightly more positive attitudes in relation to drugs than alcohol with 6 out of the 10 respondents having more positive attitudes for the drugs section than the alcohol, although such differences were small.

Table 2

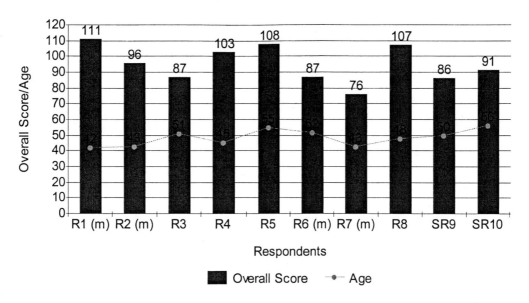

Relationship between Age and Attitudes

* Note – (m) stands for male respondents and SR stands for senior respondents

Age of respondents ranged from 42 to 56 and as can be seen from the above graph, there appeared to be no significant link as to whether a younger age (and perhaps recently qualified) related to lower scores, hence more positive attitudes.

Table 3

Relationship between Length of Time Qualified and Attitudes

LENGTH QUALIFIED	OVERALL SCORES	AVERAGE SCORES
0 – 1 Year	111	
	96	
	103	103.3
2 – 5 Years	76	
	107	91.5
6 – 10 Years	87	
	87	87
10 Years +	108	
	86	
	91	95

There did appear to be some correlation between respondents' length of time qualified and lower scores. Looking at the above table it was interesting to discover that those with the

most positive attitude were those who had been qualified between 6 and 10 years, with an average score of 87. Surprisingly those who had been qualified under a year where the ones who had the least positive average score from the four categories above, followed by those who had been qualified 10+ years.

Table 4

Respondents with Substance Misuse Training

Percentage with Alcohol Training

Not had Training (20.0%)

Had Training (80.0%)

Percentage with Drugs Training

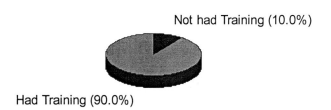

Not had Training (10.0%)

Had Training (90.0%)

Although all respondents had received either alcohol or drugs training or sometimes both, from the above Pie Charts it can be seen that fewer had been trained in alcohol issues than drugs issues. However there appeared to be no link between whether a respondent had training in both alcohol and drugs and had a lower overall score.

<u>Summary</u>

- Overall most respondents had a low score for both alcohol and drugs, suggesting a positive attitude to substance misuse.
- There appeared to be no correlation between respondents' age and a positive or negative attitude.
- There did however appear to be a relationship between length of time qualified and a positive attitude, with those being least or most qualified holding the least positive attitudes.

- Fewer respondents had been trained in alcohol than drugs, although there appeared no relationship between being trained in both and a positive score.

Findings of Interviews

The main themes emerging from the interviews are outlined below.

Knowledge and Awareness of Drug and Alcohol Use

Respondents in general appeared to lack knowledge of drug and alcohol use, although most were able to identify the health and social risks associated with substance misuse. However it was noted that the majority of respondents were more likely to recount symptoms of Neo-natal Abstinence Syndrome than Foetal Alcohol Syndrome.

'I would say my knowledge of drug use is very limited' **Respondent 1**

'There's the dangers of sharing needles...having to finance the drugs as well, they're either having to go shoplifting or prostitution.' **Respondent 6**

'Withdrawal symptoms can be quite unsettled, the baby can have the shakes and things like that...' **Respondent 4**

In terms of current knowledge of substance misuse, the majority of respondents mentioned the re-classification of cannabis and binge drinking as current debates. No one could identify the daily benchmarks for safe alcohol consumption and most respondents could not identify publications in relation to substance misuse; when they did so it was in relation to drugs; no-one mentioned alcohol.

'I'm aware of but again it's the media, is information about increasing concerns about young females and their rise in consuming alcohol...' **Respondent 1**

'I think it's only a couple of pints if you're driving isn't it?' **Respondent 7**

'Publications, never looked at them.' **Respondent 8**

With respect to the underlying causes of substance misuse most respondents could identify poverty and the fact that women may be more vulnerable due to previous abuse.

'...there was a few girls who were using Heroin and their sort of reason for using was because they had been abused as children...it was there way of shutting everything out...'
Respondent 2

'I think the drug misuse in the area we work with is primarily in your less well off areas and I think it's peer pressure, I think it's unemployment, I think it's abysmal housing...'
Respondent 6

However the overwhelming majority could not ascertain why ethnic minorities or disabled people may be more susceptible to substance misuse.

'All I can speak about ethnic minorities is all I can see on TV or even in the papers...But disability...they do say that Cannabis helps the pain...but I don't work with people who are disabled and take drugs.' **Respondent 6**

And one respondent did not think that substance misuse was an issue for those of a minority ethnic culture.

'As far as ethnic minorities are concerned, I think it's not an issue...it would be very much flying in the face of their cultural values to get involved in drug use...' **Respondent 5**

Overall most felt that they should or would like to know more in relation to substance misuse and commented on getting a lot of their knowledge from other agencies or their own experiences of drinking alcohol.

'I use my own experience of you know my community to get my kinda knowledge about alcohol and maybe a wee bit of delving into the media...but even that's not enough...I should know more.' **Respondent 2**

'If there's particular information for a particular person that you're working with that you're not sure about...you know we tend to rely on our health colleagues to give us information.' **Senior Respondent 9**

Summary

- Knowledge in general about substance misuse came across as being vague and confusing for most respondents. Although most people could identify some health and social risks in relation to substance misuse and also some underlying causes, respondents were more likely to know the symptoms relating to drug misuse than alcohol misuse and could not in general identify why minority ethnic or disabled people might be more vulnerable to misuse.
- Similarly although respondents could identify a few current debates in relation to substances, these were most often those discussed in the media. Most could not identify any publications.
- Respondents felt that they should know more about substance misuse, highlighting the need to go to other agencies for information.

Impact of Drugs and Alcohol on Children and Families

In general the majority of respondents held the view that, although they believed parents who misused substances genuinely loved their children, parenting capacity was nearly always negatively affected, commenting that when substance misuse became 'chaotic', the parents' need to find the substance overrode their responsibility to care appropriately for their child.

'I would say that a lot of the parents…do really love their kids but due to their addiction sometimes their kids just don't come first' **Respondent 4**

'To me once they start heroin whatever way, their caring abilities is compromised.' **Respondent 6**

As such respondents tended to speak of the risks children faced due to their parents' substance misuse. This ranged from risks in terms of the associates parents kept, of money being used for substances rather than basic necessities…

'In drugs the risks to children…are…people are going about the houses…you don't know what they've been up to in the past, everybody's taking drugs so there's needles, maybe kids seeing it.' **Respondent 6**

'Quite often some heroin addicts use up all the resources in the house on their addiction; money, food, everything....' **Respondents 7**

...to children having difficulties integrating with peers, achieving well academically or taking on adult responsibilities for caring for their parents/siblings when parents were under the influence. Overwhelmingly people spoke of drug misuse in this context.

'They're getting cried junkie kids in the street...that's making him angry and he wants to fight people.' **Respondent 6**

'She is an eight year old girl...her education's been affected by her not wanting to go to school by worrying about her mum.' **Respondent 3**

'The oldest lassie took on the parenting role and got all the weans out to school...' **Respondent 4**

Although respondents' stories often spoke of how children were likely to be accommodated due to their parents' substance misuse, the majority could recount positive experiences in families and therefore spoke of the value of extended families, such as grandparents, in helping children build resilience. However in general such stories tended to focus on women being lone parents and of them therefore struggling to provide stable environments for children.

'Due to her drug use and her inability to care for them, they ended up being accommodated and we are now going for permanency planning...' **Respondent 4**

'...she still has her children with her...they adore her and she adores them...the bonding in that family is amazing.' **Senior Respondent 10**

'You pray for a supportive granny...a supportive auntie or somebody who can be in there and be the stabilising factor for these children.' **Respondent 5**

As such most respondents commented on parents employing strategies to try and reduce the impact of their substance misuse on their children, although the majority still believed that once substance misuse became 'chaotic', parents' ability to use strategies diminished.

'they'll either drink when the kids are in bed or wait till they are at granny's...and they can keep substances out of the way of children – keeping needles and equipment stored.'
Respondent 3

'My experience is that when their drug use is chaotic their strategies go out of the window...they can't help themselves.' **Respondent 6**

Summary

- In general most respondents believed that parenting capacity was affected negatively by substance misuse and although they thought parents loved their children, the overwhelming majority felt that once substance misuse became 'chaotic' the parents' need for the substance overrode their need to care for their children.
- Respondents believed that children faced risks due to their parents' substance misuse and agreed that children faced further adversity due to caring responsibilities and the likelihood of being accommodated due to their parents' substance misuse. Most spoke of drugs in this context.
- However most respondents could recount positive experiences in such families with parents attempting to employ methods to minimise their substance use on children, although most agreed that such strategies failed when substance use became 'chaotic'.
- Overall stories appeared to comment on women being lone parents and fathers being absent.

Intervention and Attitudes to Substance Misuse

The majority of respondents worried about their ability to appropriately assess how substance misuse (in particular drug misuse) impacted on children, admitting that they struggled with knowing when 'good enough' parenting wasn't good enough anymore. They spoke of the difficulties in establishing trust with parents, particularly when children covered up for them and of difficulty gaining access to families.

'I don't have the experience to know what to look for...what to be concerned about...and conversely what not to be worried about...' **Respondent 1**

'There's always that grey area, you know; when is enough enough?' **Respondent 3**

'Secrecy...I suppose children will protect their parents and we're aware that they've been told not to tell the social worker what's happening and that can be difficult to cut through.' **Respondent 5**

Although the majority of respondents implied they used the Framework for Assessment of Children in Need and their Families when doing assessments, only a few respondents spoke of using interventions specific to substance misuse when intervening, with most using these due to their personal preferences rather than their effectiveness in tackling substance misuse.

'If I'm looking at assessment, see the triangle we get? I would probably more base my assessment on that...' **Respondent 7**

'I'm quite fond of using brief therapy, solution focused work...I feel most comfortable working with that...' **Respondent 3**

Similarly the majority of social workers stated that their main focus of intervention would be the children with only a minority stating that they would also include parents. Some respondents mentioned that they had dilemmas on who to focus on – the needs of the child or the needs of the parents and most believed that the best way forward for tackling parents' addiction was to refer them onto another agency to help them with their substance problem.

'The welfare of the children must come first...but that's one of the dilemmas...you think, well will I address the parents' needs...or do I address the child's?' **Respondent 1**

'The majority of our work I would say...as far as drugs and alcohol is concerned, is passing it onto other resources...I rely on other agencies to refer to...' **Respondent 4**

It was therefore noted that the overwhelming majority of workers stated that they did not feel confident in working with parental substance misuse and felt that the training given by the local authority on substance misuse was insufficient to enable them to do their job, feeling that it needed to be more in-depth.

'I wouldn't say absolutely not because I am gaining the knowledge...but I don't feel very confident.' **Respondent 1**

'I've had basic training...I think you need to go to a higher level, likes of the lassie I've got...I've learnt more from her than I've learnt in any training day on the effects, where they inject.' **Respondent 8**

In terms of attitudes, the majority of respondents recognised the value fathers played in such families, although a small minority felt that fathers had a negative influence and were often the cause of why women misused substances or perpetrators of violence in the home.

'I think in general fathers are important to family life...In one case...she was a binge drinker...The dad was really quite good at supporting mum and making sure that she was getting the appropriate help.' **Respondent 3**

'...if they have got an influence, it's usually a negative one...they're just not there or when they are there it's them that's usually supplying the mothers with drugs.' **Respondent 4**

A minority of respondents believed that along with problem substance misuse came lying and manipulation and the majority admitted that they had heard derogatory comments in the workplace directed at substance misusing parents, mostly drug using parents. However most believed that this was people's way of letting off steam as opposed to their real value base.

'I don't want to work with anymore folk with drugs problem because it's just so difficult...they'll promise you the earth and you just have to realise...you cannae take anything that's said at face value.' **Respondent 5**

'It can be really quite stressful and folk need to be able to let that out...in a non kinda social work way...they don't generally view it like that tho.' **Respondent 4**

Nearly all respondents felt supported at work from their senior and felt confident in approaching them for advice on substance misuse and parenting.

'I've got really good support from my senior...and if they don't know, you are pointed in the right direction to get the right information.' **Respondent 3**

Summary

- Overall respondents worried about being able to assess in families where there was parental substance misuse due to the difficulty of knowing when someone was under the influence of substances, of establishing what 'good enough' parenting was and of the barriers they faced with regards to engaging with families.

- Most respondents said they assessed such families using the Framework for Assessment of Children in Need and their Families but in general were unsure of interventions with only a few mentioning attempting to use those specific to substance misuse. The majority of respondents felt that referring parents to another agency was best to deal with their substance misuse and admitted that their main focus of intervention would be children, with only a few stating they would include parents.

- In terms of attitudes most social workers agreed about the important role fathers played in such families, although some disagreed. The majority admitted that although they had heard derogatory comments in the workplace towards such families, that it was just a way of venting off their feelings of frustration, not their true values. However a minority of social workers believed that alongside substance misuse came lying and manipulation from service users.

- Most respondents felt supported in the workplace.

- Overall the majority did not feel confident in their role when working with substance misusing parents and their children. Although the majority had training in substance misuse, most felt that it wasn't enough to carry out their role and felt it needed to be more in-depth.

V

COMMENT AND CRITIQUE OF THE OUTCOME OF FINDINGS

As aforementioned, triangulation was used to corroborate the findings from the research (Denscombe 2003). This process revealed three distinct areas that arose as being relevant from both the quantitative and qualitative methods used which are discussed below.

Knowledge and confidence in working with families experiencing parental substance misuse.

From the findings of the questionnaires and interviews it would appear that respondents did not feel adequately prepared for their role in terms of having adequate knowledge and skills to carry out their roles as social workers with families experiencing parental substance misuse. Although the results of the questionnaires in terms of overall scores revealed that respondents had slightly more positive scores with drugs than alcohol, when broken down into individual sections the questionnaires revealed that social workers appeared to feel more confident in their knowledge of alcohol use as opposed to drugs, but perhaps surprisingly stated feeling more competent about the causes and risks of drug misuse rather than alcohol misuse.

Similarly knowledge about substances appeared to be patchy throughout the interviews and although the majority of respondents could identify health and social risks in relation to substance misuse, the overall majority were more likely to know the symptoms of neo-natal abstinence syndrome than foetal alcohol syndrome. Furthermore from the findings of the interviews it was apparent that most respondents associated substance misuse with *drug use* with most referring to drug use when talking about cases and it was also apparent from respondents' accounts that they felt more comfortable with alcohol issues than drugs. Therefore such findings could be found to suggest that social workers tended to focus on the risk elements of substance misuse, which was supported in their accounts in interviews when they spoke of the risks children faced such as problems with school, issues in the community and the increased likelihood of children being accommodated.

Such themes were evident in the Scottish Executive (2001:1) publication, *'Getting Our Priorities Right'* which claimed *'parental use may have significant and damaging consequences for children'* and could be compared with McKeller & Coggan's (1997)

study which found that children whose parents misused substances often faced poor educational outcomes due to being socialised into such families. Furthermore these findings may reflect the fact that as aforementioned, many government publications and information appears to have focused disproportionately on drug misuse rather than alcohol misuse (ACMD 2000; Scottish Executive 2001, 2002) and would support Sloan's (1998) observations that many agencies buy into the idea that children whose parents use drugs are at risk. Furthermore, the discovery that social workers appeared to be more confident in working with alcohol misuse rather than drug misuse would reflect the findings in Forrester's (2000) research on the correlation between parental substance misuse and child protection. He ascertained that social workers had a familiarity with alcohol use, due to their own use of it but lacked knowledge in heroin use and thus often saw heroin use as *the* cause of the problem, rather than a contributing factor.

The outcomes from the interviews suggested that most social workers could not identify publications with regards to substance misuse and although they knew of a few current debates and appreciated why women and young people may be more vulnerable to substance misuse, the overwhelming majority of respondents failed to recognise why ethnic minorities or disabled people may be more susceptible to misusing substances. Indeed one respondent believed that substance misuse was not an issue for those of minority ethnic cultures.

The debates the respondents seemed to recount were those most notably publicised in the media (www.drugscope.org.uk; www.news.bbc.co.uk). The fact that social workers recognised why women may be more vulnerable to substance misuse directly agreed with Greenfield et al's (2003) and Neale's (2004) research which argued that women had a shorter progression into substance misuse than men, and that this was compounded by the fact that women often had additional pressures such as childcare responsibilities and reliance on state benefits.

However worryingly, the fact that most social workers could not identify why groups such as ethnic minorities and disabled people may be more vulnerable to substance misuse contradicted studies by Li & Ford (1998), Dyter & Mitchell (2003) and Bakshi et al (2004) who discovered that drug and alcohol use amongst such groups was certainly prevalent. Indeed these studies acknowledged how such groups' reasons for using substances was often the same for the general population; that is, to fit in, peer pressure etc and advocated that service provision needed to be sensitive to the cultural and language needs of such

communities. However as such studies highlighted the stigma associated with using substances in certain cultures and communities meant that such groups tended to hide substance use and the literature reported difficulties in sourcing research in this area; it is perhaps not surprising then that social workers may predictably lack such information.

In terms of having enough knowledge, it was also evident from analysis of the questionnaire scores against nominal data that there was a direct link between length of time qualified and a more positive attitude to substance misuse. Those who had been qualified under a year and those who had been qualified over 10 years, held the least positive attitudes towards substance misuse. Furthermore despite nominal data from questionnaires indicating that all respondents had either received alcohol or drugs training, respondents in the interviews highlighted that training was not in-depth enough to support them in their role with respondents feeling they should know more and should not be relying on other agencies for information.

Research carried out by Watson et al (2004) into the experiences of health and social care staff would support such findings as they found that confidence amongst professionals in terms of their knowledge of substances was low, and may concur with Duffy et al's (1995) research who found that whilst training increased social workers' knowledge and confidence in their role, such knowledge diminished when not nurtured in the work environment. We could then perhaps speculate that social workers who have been qualified longest may have the least knowledge or positive attitude. It was therefore felt that the findings from both the questionnaires and interviews showed that Role Adequacy (that is confidence in having the knowledge and skills to do their job) was effectively low for most respondents, with most feeling ill equipped with knowledge to carry out their role.

Feelings about their social work role with families experiencing parental substance misuse.

In terms of feeling comfortable and responsible for certain aspects of their role, the questionnaire revealed that respondents would feel comfortable asking service users about their drug misuse; however the majority suggested that they would feel more comfortable doing this with regard to alcohol use. In this respect participants' work satisfaction and self esteem was low in general, appearing more so with drugs as the majority of respondents felt it more rewarding to work with alcohol misuse than drug misuse. As such the questionnaires revealed that respondents' Role Legitimacy (that is the extent to which

they feel they have the right to intervene) appeared lower with regards to drug misuse rather than alcohol misuse.

Again respondents' lack of Role Legitimacy and right to intervene appeared to be supported in the findings of the interviews. The fact that the questionnaires highlighted that social workers had low work satisfaction with those who misuse substance, may be tentatively applied to the findings of the interviews whereby respondents spoke of the difficulties in making assessments in such families. Most respondents spoke of trying to apply the Framework for Assessment of Children in Need and their Families to give structure to assessments but also spoke of facing difficulties in terms of knowing if someone was under the influence of substances, of deciding what was 'good enough' parenting and of barriers to assessment such as parents avoiding contact with agencies or children covering up for parents, all of which made the task of assessment more difficult. However despite this, most respondents interviewed stated that they felt supported in the workplace by their senior.

Research such as Barnard & Barlow (2003) and Kroll (2004) echoed such findings by speaking about how children would often cover up for parents and be secretive to authority figures that entered their home by refusing to disclose parental substance misuse. Similarly research by Kroll & Taylor (2003; 2004) showed how social workers worried about knowing what was *'good enough'* parenting and of over/under reacting with families and also spoke of difficulties in engaging with parents when they feared what intervention from social services would bring.

Throughout the interviews respondents struggled with deciding on who to focus on - the child or the parents - and generally lacked confidence in intervening. Most respondents were unsure of what method of intervention they should use and the majority highlighted that the best course of action to deal with a parents' substance misuse problem would be to refer them onto other agencies. This was also echoed in the findings of the questionnaire when most respondents stated that they were unsure whether the best they could do was to refer someone onto other agencies. Such findings would be supported by Hayden (2004) who argued that social workers felt out of their depth in understanding the needs of substance misusing parents and how to intervene and would conflict with Kroll & Taylor (2003:284) who noted the suitability of using the cycle of change and motivational interviewing to effect change in those who misused substances.

It was therefore recognised that the overall findings from the interviews would support those of the questionnaires with regards to Role Adequacy and Role Legitimacy. The overwhelming majority of respondents in the interviews and questionnaires showed a distinct lack of confidence in their role with parents who misused substances and their children and in this respect, both Role Adequacy and Legitimacy amongst respondents was lowered.

Attitudes in relation to families where parental substance misuse exists.

Although in general in the interviews most social workers believed that fathers were important in such families and should be included, a minority argued that in their experience fathers had a negative influence on families by often introducing women to drugs, being the perpetrators of violence and often absent from families. Such findings would concur with Frank et al's (2002) study who noted that fathers who misused substances were less likely to be involved in raising their children and more likely to be absent. However the findings would also agree with those of McMahon & Rounsville's (1997) review of the literature who found that fathers often wanted to be as involved in their children's lives as women, and could be a source of support to mothers. Interestingly the overwhelmingly majority of respondents spoke of women in their accounts of substance misuse and parenting which may reflect the disproportionate number of studies which have focused on mothering and substance misuse (Nair et al 1997; McKeganey et al 2002).

In terms of being motivated towards working with those who misused substances, most respondents from the questionnaires showed a positive attitude towards this. However it was worthy to note that respondents stated they were more motivated to finding out more about drug misuse rather than alcohol misuse but again seemed to lack confidence in intervening with drug using families. What was interesting was the fact that despite questionnaires in general denoting a positive attitude to substance misuse, the interview findings did not always support this. Although the majority of social workers in the interviews could recount positive experiences in such families; for example, the bond apparent in such families and of parents employing strategies to keep their children safe from their substances; a minority of respondents in the interviews believed that along with substance misuse comes lying and manipulation. Furthermore in interviews the majority of social workers believed that parenting capacity was nearly always negatively affected by parental substance misuse and believed that often 'chaotic' substance use would mean that

the parent's needs for drugs overrode their need to care appropriately for their children, perhaps suggesting a less positive attitude. However in the same respect, respondents did speak of how extended family members, especially grandparents, acted as a buffer for children when living with parents who had substance misuse problems.

Such findings would match research by Nair et al (1997), Hogan (1998) and Klee (1998) who found that parental substance misuse and poor parenting was not always a definite outcome. A study by Barker & Carson (1999) of substance misusing women found that women attempted to employ strategies such as reducing their substance intake when children were around in order to protect them. However the majority of social workers agreeing that once substance misuse became *'chaotic'* parents' ability to employ such strategies and care of their children was reduced, complemented studies carried out by McKeganey et al (2002); Barnard & McKeganey (2003) and Hayden (2004) who found that the scale of parental substance misuse directly affected parents' ability to parent and as such that most parents' needs for substances overrode the need to care for their children. However the fact that family members provided a protective factor for children was echoed in research by Marcenko et al (2000) and Barnard (2005). The finding that a minority of social workers thought that with substance misuse came with lying and manipulation would match Klee (1998) review of past research where she found that judgemental views of drug using parents existed between the public and professionals.

The fact that the respondents in the questionnaires claimed to be interested in the nature of drug misuse more than alcohol misuse, appeared to be challenged in the interviews. Although in general social workers claimed in both interviews and questionnaires that they understood the underlying reasons as to why people misused substances, such as poverty and past sexual abuse and thus appreciated that it wasn't simply a matter of individual choice, respondents in the interviews admitted to hearing derogatory comments in the workplace and although most felt that this was just a way of 'venting off' frustrations, most mentioned from their stories that the comments were directed at drug users. This would correspond with studies from Plant et al (2005) and Meier et al (1999) who discovered that poverty, deprivation and disadvantage were common features in the lives of those who misused substances and Turnnard (2002b) who also noted that histories of sexual abuse was also prevalent amongst such groups. However the fact that derogatory comments were noted may be similar to the attitudes outlined in Hayden (2004) study where social workers admitted that they did not have much faith in such parents changing.

In terms of motivation, self-esteem and work satisfaction respondents in general appeared more motivated to work with those who misused alcohol than drugs and thus felt more assured and rewarding to work with those who misused alcohol. It may therefore be appropriate to speculate that the findings from both the questionnaire and interviews would perhaps concur with Shaw et al (1978) (cited in Watson et al 2003) who claimed that when Role Adequacy and Role Legitimacy was low, motivation, self-esteem and work satisfaction would also be low. In conjunction from the above it would appear that Role Adequacy and Legitimacy were lower in relation to drug misuse than alcohol misuse and hence respondents had lower motivation, self-esteem and work satisfaction in working with such service users.

As such the findings appear to support the original hypothesis of the study which expected to find that social workers may experience difficulties in working with parental substance misuse and may thus develop poor attitudes/motivation towards such service users.

VI

SUMMARY AND CONCLUSIONS

This research has revealed a wealth of experiences on parental substance misuse from social workers in a children and families setting. This is perhaps hardly surprising given the complexities involved in parental substance misuse and indeed the Scottish Executive's (2001) expected response from social workers to the issue.

The most apparent themes that arose from the research were the fact that the overwhelming majority of the social workers that took part in the study did not feel that they had the appropriate knowledge and skills to adequately fulfil their role, meaning that they did not therefore feel confident in their role with such families and although in general attitudes were positive, some attitudes showed discriminatory attitudes towards parents who misused substances. As aforementioned such findings concurred with Shaw (1978) (cited in Watson et al 2003) who noted that if knowledge and skills were low, so too would be workers' feelings and attitudes towards such client groups. These findings may therefore have significant implications for practice, particularly in relation to assessment and intervention, not only for those involved in the study but similarly if such findings are found to represent the thoughts and feelings of others in the field.

Firstly if social workers lack the appropriate knowledge and skills for the post, one could argue that their opportunity to conduct holistic assessments (which is the expected standard from the Scottish Executive) may thus be limited (Scottish Executive 2001). This could be further evidenced with the majority of social workers in interviews admitting that they were on the whole unaware of publications about substance misuse and as such would perhaps raise questions about the basis on which assessments were being formed. Middleton (1997:5) (cited in Adams 2002:5) reminds us that assessment should be underpinned by a strong theoretical framework and it could then be argued that future interventions may not be appropriate or indeed dangerous; as Thompson (2000b:140) asserts *'a mistake or oversight at the assessment stage can lead to significant difficulties later on...'*

Similarly social workers' lack of awareness of why vulnerable groups such as disabled service users or ethnic minority service users may be more susceptible to substance misuse, may have implications in terms of how the local authority can meet the requirements of the

49

Race Relations (Amendment) Act 2000 to have ethnically sensitive practices in place (www.scotland.gov.uk) and indeed how social workers fulfil their duty under the Children (Scotland) Act 1995 to take into account children's racial origin or cultural needs (Norrie 1998:59). Thompson (2000b:134) reminds us that if we fail to be aware of issues of inequality then we run the risk of adding to or exacerbating the oppression they already face and in this respect social workers face the possibility of not meeting the requirements of the Social Work Code of Practice that stipulates that they must respect and value diversity (SSSC 2003:Code 1.6).

The attitudes or views that social workers held may also implicate practice. Thompson (2001:70) argues that *'if the social worker has stereotypical expectations and attitudes he or she will tend to select information to confirm them'* and as such the social workers in the study run the risk of pre-judging such families or even excluding members from the assessment and intervention process. By being unsure about whether to include fathers/parents in assessments, believing that lying is a pre-requisite of substance misuse or that parenting capacity is nearly always negatively affected, we may reasonably question the extent to which such views are conducive with social workers' responsibility to work in partnership with parents (Norrie 1998; Protecting Children 1998; Scottish Executive 2001), their duty under the s22 of Children (Scotland) Act 1995 to promote a child's upbringing by their family (Norrie 1998:59) or indeed the extent to which they could establish a trusting relationship on which to base successful intervention (Thompson 2000b:78).

The fact that findings showed that social workers involved in the research felt more confident in their knowledge of alcohol misuse but tended to focus on the risks children faced in relation to parental drug misuse, may effectively support the argument that intervention can become too narrow focused, concentrating on minimising risk and failing to take a holistic view, which may then place doubt on the extent to which they can employ the Framework for Assessment of Children in Need and their Families or indeed take part in effective joint-working. Such polarised views have been the criticism of many public enquiries regarding social worker's practice (www.edinburgh.gov.uk) and could mean that social workers associate drug use as *the* factor placing children at risk, perhaps failing to consider that *'it is the accumulation of risk factors that jeopardises development ...'* (Garbarino 1995:157) or appreciate how structural factors such as poverty/deprivation play a part in such children's lives.

In this respect it is evident that perhaps such attitudes may negatively affect practice as Watson et al (2003:4) highlight, *'the attitudes...professionals hold towards...individuals...impact on the quality of care delivered'* and as such it could be argued that social workers who hold such views may not be able to practice the core values of social work to *'respect and value uniqueness and diversity...'* (Banks 2001:62) or support a client/worker relationship which is based on the central social work value of *'unconditional positive regard'* (Thompson 2000b:114).

Such issues may correlate with the fact that the majority of social workers interviewed divulged that they felt that the level of training currently offered by the local authority on substance misuse was not sufficient to carry out their roles. This may have implications for practice in the sense that if training needs are not being addressed sufficiently, not only may the organisation be failing in their duty under the Social Work Code of Practice to *'support staff to address deficiencies in their performance'* (SSSC 2003:Code 2.2) but also that social workers will continue to have poor knowledge; as Watson et al (2003) discovered poor attitudes often lead to the extent to which knowledge is accepted and practised also being poor.

As Chubb & Thompson (2000:3) note *'all social work takes place in an organisational context'*; it is worth highlighting how such findings may not only impact on the organisation's culture in the present but may also impact on future practice. Therefore considering the findings in the wider context of the future of social work and specifically in relation to the recent Scottish Executive's *'21st Century Social Work Review'*, which outlines the role of social work in the future with regards to expectations and standards, was deemed appropriate (Scottish Executive 2006).

The review expects social workers to *'be able to explain and account for their practice, basing their decisions...on the basis of sound assessment and robust evidence of what works'* (Scottish Executive 2006). Therefore in terms of future practice, if social workers currently lack knowledge or are unaware of current research in the field of substance misuse and families, they run the danger of not meeting this need and of not applying evidence-based practice to inform assessments.

Similarly, if social workers lack knowledge or appreciation of why certain groups in society may be more vulnerable to substance misuse, are unsure of the usefulness of family members in processes or are indeed unsure of who to focus intervention on, they face the

real possibility of falling short of the major aim of the Review to promote *'inclusiveness...by enabling some of our most vulnerable...to play an active part in society...'* and questions whether in the future they will be able to *'work alongside people to help them build resilience...and develop their strengths and abilities'* (Scottish Executive 2006).

Finally what is important to highlight is that if social workers do not feel confident in their role with such families and as a result practice in a manner that perhaps focuses on risk, particularly in relation to drug misuse, the implications for future practice may mean that the service would be operating contrary to the Review's intention to focus on early intervention, based on planned assessment and in this sense practice may be more reactive rather than proactive (Scottish Executive 2006).

Therefore in conclusion, consideration has to be given to the themes arising from the research not only in terms of how they implicate practice in the present but also in the future. In general if social workers are not trained to the level *they* feel they need to do their job, do not feel as if *they* can make a difference and feel as if *they* are constantly *'swimming against the tide'* (Adams 2002), it is debatable whether they will achieve the 21st Century Social Work Reviews' overall aim of having a social work which can change in a way that allows workers to be responsive to individuals by promoting their participation and taking a user-centred approach (Scottish Executive 2006).

In this sense, although the researcher felt that the methodology applied in this study was successful for the intended purpose, it is essential that social workers' thoughts and views are listened to and also put into action and therefore it is felt that perhaps an area of future research would be a purely qualitative study which explored social workers' feelings after they received the type of training and support *they* feel they needed. It is also worth acknowledging that there is a distinct lack of research with regards to ethnic minorities, disabled people and men who misuse substances and therefore research in this area would also help inform future practice. In this respect, if such research were carried out perhaps then social workers' views and Scottish Executive expectations would be more congruent with each other and may repair the current gaps in social workers' knowledge in relation to substance misuse.

REFERENCES

Adams R, Dominelli L and Payne M (2002) (2nd Ed) <u>Social Work: Themes, Issues & Critical Debates.</u> Palgrave: Basingstoke

Advisory Council on the Misuse of Drugs (ACMD) (2000) <u>Hidden Harm: Responding to the needs of children of drug users.</u> The Stationery Office:London

Alcock (1997) (2nd Ed) <u>Understanding Poverty.</u> Macmillan: Basingstoke

Alston M & Bowles W (2003) (2nd Ed) <u>Research for Social Workers: An Introduction to Methods.</u> Routledge: London

Baillie D, Cameron K, Cull L, Roche J & West J (2003) (Ed) <u>Social Work & the Law in Scotland.</u> Palgrave Macmillan: Basingstoke

Bakshi N, Ross A, Heim D, Bakshi N, Flately K, Hunter S, Mahal N & Tordzro K (2004) <u>Drug and Alcohol Issues Affecting Pakistani, Indian and Chinese Young People and their Communities: A Study in Greater Glasgow, August 2002, Final Report.</u> Greater Glasgow NHS Board

Banks S (2001) (2nd Ed) <u>Ethics & Values in Social Work.</u> Palgrave: Basingstoke

Barber JG (2002) (2nd Ed) <u>Social Work with Addictions.</u> Palgrave Macmillan: Basingstoke

Barker PL & Carson A (1999) <u>'I Take Care of My Kids': Mothering Practices of Substance-Abusing Women.</u> Gender & Society, Vol 13, No3, June 1999 pp 347-363

Barnard M (2003) <u>Between a Rock and a Hard Place: the Role of Relatives in Protecting Children from the Effects of Parental Drug Problems.</u> Child and Family Social Work 2003, Vol 8, pp 291-299

Barnard M (2005) <u>Drugs in the Family: The Impact on Parents and Siblings.</u> www.jrf.org.uk/bookshop/ebooks

Barnard M & Barlow J (2003) <u>Discovering Parental Drug Dependence: Silence and Disclosure.</u> Children & Society, Vol 17, 2003, pp 45-56

Barnard M & McKeganey N (2003) <u>The Impact of Parental Problem Drug Use on Children: What is the Problem and What can be done to Help?</u> Addiction 99, pp 552-559

Chubb T & Thompson N (2000) <u>Working in Organisations.</u> Prospects Publications: Wrexham

Corby B (1996) 'Risk Assessment in Child Protection Work' cited in Kemshall H & Pritchard J (1996) <u>Good Practice in Risk Assessment & Risk Management 1.</u> Jessica Kingsley: London

Corwall A & Jewkes R (1995) <u>What is Participatory Research?</u> Social Science and Medicine, 41, pp 1667-1676

D'Cruz H and Jones M (2004) <u>Social Work Research: Ethical and Political Contexts.</u> SAGE Publications Ltd: London

Department of Health (DOH) (2000) <u>Statistical Bulletin: Statistics from the Regional Drug Misuse Database for six months ending March 2000.</u> DOH: London

Denscombe M (2003) (2nd Ed) <u>The Good Research Guide: For Small-scale Social Research Projects.</u> Open University Press: Berkshire

Duffy T, Holttum S & Keegan M (1998) <u>An Investigation of the Impact of Training Social Workers and their Managers.</u> Journal of Alcoholism, 1998; 34 (1-2) pp 93-104

DrugScope (2002) <u>Annual Report on the UK Drug Situation 2001.</u> DrugScope: London

Dyter R & Mitchell T (2003) <u>Drug Misuse Amongst People with Disabilities: A Scoping Study.</u> www.drugs.gov.uk/publications

Egan G (2002) (7th Ed) <u>The Skilled Helper.</u> Pacific, CA: BrooksCole

Every Child Matters (2003) HMSO: Norwich <u>www.everychildmatters.gov.uk/publications</u>

Forrester D (2000) <u>Parental Substance Misuse and Child Protection in a British Sample: A Survey of Children on the Child Protection Register in an Inner London District Office.</u> Child Abuse Review, Vol 9 pp 235-246

Fountain J, Dr, Bashford J & Winters M (2003) <u>Black and Minority Ethnic Communities in England: a review of the literature on drug use and related service provision.</u> University of Central Lancashire. National Treatment Agency for Substance Misuse/Centre for Ethnicity & Health: London
www.nta.nhs.uk/publications/bme_lit.pdf

Frank DA, Brown J, Johnson S & Cabral H (2002) <u>Forgotten Fathers: An Exploratory Study of Mothers' Report of Drug and Alcohol Problems Among Fathers of Urban Newborns.</u> Neurotoxicology and Teratology 24 (2002) 339 - 347

Garbarino J (1995) <u>Raising Children in a Socially Toxic Environment.</u> Jossey-Bass: California

Gossop M (2000) (5th Ed) <u>Living with Drugs.</u> Ashgate Publishing: Aldershot

Greenfield SF, Manwani SG & Nargiso JE (2003) <u>Epidemiology of Substance use Disorders in Women.</u> Obstetrics & Gynecology Clinics of North America
www.nta.nhs.co.uk

Handy C (1993) (4th Ed) <u>Understanding Organisations.</u> Penguin Group: London

Hay G, Gannon M, McKeganey N, Hutchinson S & Goldberg D (2004) <u>Estimating the National and Local Prevalence of Problem Drug Misuse in Scotland.</u> Centre for Drug Misuse Research, University of Glasgow Scottish Centre for Infection and Environmental Health

Hayden C (2004) <u>Parental Substance Misuse and Child Care Social Work: Research in a City Social Work Department in England.</u> Child Abuse Review, Vol 13, 18-20

Hogan DM (1998) <u>Annotation: The Psychological Development and Welfare of Children of Opiate and Cocaine Users: Review and Research Needs.</u> Journal of Child Psychology & Psychiatry 39 (5) 609-620

Howe D (1995) <u>Attachment Theory For Social Work Practice.</u> Palgrave: Basingstoke

Kandel D (1990) <u>Parenting Styles, drug use and children's adjustment in families of young adults.</u> Journal of Marriage and the Family, 52, pp183-96

Kearney P, Levin E & Rosen G (2000) <u>Working with Families: Alcohol, Drug and Mental Health Problems.</u> National Institute of Social Work: London
Kemshall H & Pritchard J (1996) <u>Good Practice in Risk Assessment & Risk Management 1.</u> Jessica Kingsley: London

Klee, H (1998) <u>Drug-using Parents: Analysing the Stereotypes.</u> International Journal of Drug Policy, Vol 9 pp 437-448

Kroll B & Taylor A (2003) <u>Parental Substance Misuse & Child Welfare.</u> Jessica Kingsley: London

Kroll B (2004) <u>Living with an Elephant: Growing up with Parental Substance Misuse.</u> Children & Family Social Work 2004, 9, pp 129-140

Kumar R (1996) <u>Research Methodology: A Step-By-Step Guide for Beginners.</u> Sage Publications: Thousand Oaks

Li Li & Ford J (1998) <u>Illicit Drug Use by Women with Disabilitites.</u> American Journal of Drug and Alcohol Abuse, August 1998 www.findarticles.com

Marcenko M, Kemp SP & Larson NC (2000) <u>Childhood Experiences of Abuse, Later Substance Use and Parenting among Low-income Families.</u> American Journal of Orthopsychiatry, 70, pp 316-326

Marlow C (2001) <u>Research Methods for Generalist Social Work.</u> Wadsworth: Belmont CA

May T (1993) <u>Social Research: Issues, Methods and Process.</u> Open University Press: Buckingham

May T (2001) (3rd Ed) <u>Social Research: Issues, Methods and Process.</u> Open University Press: Buckingham

May M, Page R & Brunsdon E (2001) (Ed) <u>Understanding Social Problems: Issues in Social Policy.</u> Blackwell Publishers: Oxford

McKeganey N, Barnard M & McIntosh J (2002) <u>Paying the Price for their Parents' Addiction: Meeting the Needs of the Children of Drug-using Parents.</u> Drugs: Education, Prevention & Policy Vol 9, No 3

McKellar S & Coggans N (1997) <u>Responding to Family Problems, Alcohol and Substance Misuse: A Survey Provision in the Glasgow Area.</u> Children & Society Journal, Vol 11, pp 53-59

McInnes K & Newman T (2005) <u>Substance Misusing Parents and their Children.</u> Barnardo's/Safer South Gloucestershire Report www.barnardos.org.uk

McMahon & Rounsville (1997) <u>Substance Abuse and Fathering: Adding Poppa to the Research Agenda.</u> Addiction 97, pp 1109-1115

Meier PS, Donmall MC & McElduff P (2004) <u>Characteristics of Drug Users Who do or do Not have Care of their Children.</u> Addiction 99, 995-961

Miller WR & Rollnick S (2002) (2nd Ed) <u>Motivational Interviewing: Preparing People for Change.</u> Guilford: New York

Morse JM & Richards L (2002) <u>Read Me First for a User's Guide to Qualitative Methods.</u> Sage Publications: California

Murray J & Hogarth E (2003) <u>Children Affected by Substance Misuse in the Family: An Assessment of the Nature and Prevalence in the Borders.</u> Borders Drug & Alcohol Action Team cited in <u>www.drugmisuse.isdscotland.org/dat/borders/bordersChildNA.pdf</u>

Nair P, Black MM, Schuler M, Keane V, Snow L & Rigney BA (1997) <u>Risk Factors For Disruption in Primary Caregiving Among Infants of Substance Abusing Women.</u> Child Abuse & Neglect, Vol 21, No 11 pp1039 – 1051

Neale J (2004) <u>Gender & Illicit Drug Use.</u> British Journal of Social Work (2004) 34, 851-870

Norrie K Mck (1998) (Rev Ed) <u>Greens Annotated Acts: Children (Scotland) Act 1995.</u> W.Green & Son: Edinburgh

Payne M (1997) (2nd Ed) <u>Modern Social Work Theory.</u> Palgrave: Basingstoke

Plant M, Miller P & Plant M (2005) <u>The Relationship between Alcohol Consumption and Problem Behaviours: Gender Differences among British Adults.</u> Journal of Substance Use, February 2005, 10(1): 22-30

Protecting Children (1998) <u>A Shared Responsibility: Guidance on Interagency Co-operation. The Scottish Office.</u> HMSO: Edinburgh

Raymond, M (1996) <u>Research Made Simple: A Handbook for Social Workers.</u> SAGE Publications Ltd: London

Scottish Executive (2001) <u>Getting Our Priorities Right: Policy and Practice Guidelines for Working with Children and Families affected by Problem Drug Use.</u>

Scottish Executive (2002) <u>It's Everyone's Job to Make Sure I'm Alright: Report of the Child Protection Audit and Review.</u> The Stationery Office: Edinburgh

Scottish Executive (2003) <u>National Investigation into Drug Related Deaths in Scotland, 2003.</u> Substance Misuse Research: Edinburgh

Scottish Executive (2005) <u>Drugs Misuse Attitudes Survey – 2004 Post-Campaign Evaluation.</u> Scottish Executive Social Research 2005

Scottish Executive (2006) <u>Changing Lives: Report of the 21st Century Social Work Review.</u> Scottish Executive: Edinburgh www.21csocialwork.org.uk

Scottish Social Services Council (SSSC) (2003) Codes of Practice: For Social Service Workers and Employers. Scottish Social Services Council: Dundee

Silverman, D (2000) Doing Qualitative Research: A Practical Handbook. SAGE Publications Ltd: London

Sloan M (1998) Substance Misuse and Child Maltreatment. Social Work Monographs: University of East Anglia Norwich

Smale G, Tuson G & Stratham D (2000) Social Work and Social Problems: Working Towards Social Inclusion & Social Change. Palgrave: Basingstoke

Street K, Harrington J, Chiang W, Cairns P & Ellis M (2004) How Great is the Risk of Abuse in Infants born to Drug-Using Mothers. Blackwell Publishing Ltd

Tackling Drugs in Scotland: Action in Partnership (1999) The Scottish Office www.scotland.gov.uk

Taylor A & Kroll B (2004) Working with Parental Substance Misuse: Dilemmas for Practice. British Journal of Social Work, Vol 34, pp 1115-1132

Thom B (2003) Risk-taking Behaviour in Men: Substance Use and Gender. NHS Health Development Agency www.nda.online.org.uk/documents/men_at_risk_01-04-03.pdf

Thompson N (2000a) Theory and Practice in Human Services. Open University Press: Berkshire

Thompson N (2000b) Understanding Social Work: Preparing for Practice. Palgrave: Basingstoke

Thompson N (2001) (3rd Ed) Anti-Discriminatory Practice. Palgrave: Basingstoke

Trevithivk P (2000) Social Work Skills: A Practice Handbook. Open University Press: Buckingham

Turnnard J (2002a) Research in Practice: Parental Problem Drinking and it's Impact on Children. www.rip.org.uk/publications/documents/researchreviews/ALCOHOL.pdf

Turnnrd J (2002b) Research in Practice: Parental Drug Misuse – A Review of Impact and Intervention Studies. www.rip.org.uk/publications

Watson H, Maclaren W, Shaw F, Nolan A (2003) Measuring Staff Attitudes to People with Drug Problems: The Development of a Tool. Effective Interventions Unit. Scottish Executive Drug Misuse Research Programme . www.drugmisuse.isdscotland.org/publications/eiupublications

Watson H, Girvan M, Kelly T, Kerr S, Hislop J, Thow M, Dickson R & Coull S (2004) Drug and Alcohol Training Needs of Generic Health and Social Care Staff. Caledonian University Nursing & Midwifery Research Centre, September 2004

Yin RK (1994) Case Study Research: Design and Methods. Sage Publications: Thousand Oaks

Websites:

www.adoptionuk.com
www.alcohol-focus-scotland.org.uk
www.basw.co.uk
www.drugscope.org.uk
www.drugs.gov.uk
www.edinburgh.gov.uk
www.edinburgh.gov.uk/socialwork/calebness/calebness.html
www.hebs.scot.nhs.uk
www.isdscotland.org
www.news.bbc.co.uk
www.unison-scotland.org.uk
www.scotland.gov.uk
www.scotland.gov.uk/library/documents-w7/tdis-01.htm
www.show.scot.nhs.uk